A gift for

_____

From

_____

Buddy Up!

Copyright © 2010 by Simon & Schuster, Inc.

This edition published in 2011 by Hallmark Gift Books,
a division of Hallmark Cards, Inc.,
Kansas City, MO 64141
Visit us on the Web at www.Hallmark.com.

All rights reserved, including the right to reproduce this book or portions thereof in any form whatsoever. For information address Gallery Books Subsidiary Rights Department, 1230 Avenue of the Americas, New York, NY 10020.

Designed by Jaime Putorti

ISBN: 978-1-59530-465-0
BOK3131

Printed and bound in the United States

Buddy Up!

Friend. Compadre. Chum. Pal. Buddy.

Friendship is a natural part of life. After all, we're social animals. Plus, having friends around makes everything more fun—you have someone to talk to, someone you can trust, someone who will be there for you when you need a helping hand.

But do you know what's even better than having a friend?

Having a buddy.

A *buddy* is someone who will have your back, who's always looking out for you and you're responsible for looking out for in return. A buddy goes on adventures, road trips, and snack runs. A buddy never judges. A buddy gives the best hugs. A buddy tells you if you have food in your teeth.

We invite you to take a moment to think about your best buds as you read about the amazing true friendships celebrated on the pages that follow. And later, as you head out into the world and face countless unknowns and embark on amazing exploits, don't forget what our kindergarten teachers and camp counselors taught us: Life's better when we Buddy Up!

Buddies know that two heads are better than one.

A chimpanzee named Anjana gives his best bud, a white tiger cub, a boost. Anjana helps the cub's human keeper care for the baby tiger at an endangered animal sanctuary in Myrtle Beach, South Carolina.

Buddies always stick together.

Ulrok, an eighteen-month-old Rottweiler, adopted Beldaran, an eight-week-old wolf, after she was rejected by her parents. The buddies, both rescue animals, romp and play at the Kisma Preserve in Mount Desert, Maine.

Buddies help you search for snacks.

Tonda, an orangutan, gives some food to his best friend, T.K. (short for Tonda's Kitty), at Zoo World in Panama City, Florida. T.K. was given to Tonda after the orangutan's constant companion passed away, and now the two are rarely apart.

Buddies know that good fences make good *neighhh*bors.

A spaniel sits next to a pony at a farm in West Devonshire, England. The dog and the pony have been lifelong friends and they enjoy playing, eating, and guarding the farm's fences together.

Buddies understand that everything's better with bacon.

Abandoned by its mother, this tiger cub was adopted by a sow and enjoys playing with its piglet siblings in a park in Guangdong, China.

Buddies aren't afraid to mix fur with snakeskin—it looks fabulous!

A hamster was given to a snake as a meal, but Aochan the rat snake refused to eat his new friend. Now the two live in the same cage in a zoo in Tokyo, Japan, and the hamster sometimes falls asleep on top of his natural predator. Zookeepers nicknamed the hamster Gohan, a Japanese word that means "meal."

(Koichi Kamoshida/Getty Images)

Buddies know that sometimes it's good to have friends in high places.

Bella the dog sits beneath her best friend Tarra, an Asian elephant, at The Elephant Sanctuary in Hohenwald, Tennessee. Bella was a stray who lived at the sanctuary when she met Tarra, and the two have since bonded.

(Melanie Stetson Freeman/Christian Science Monitor/Getty Images)

Buddies make hump days more pleasant.

Tatenda the rhino and Poggles the warthog take a leisurely stroll near their home in Zimbabwe. The two exotic beasts have known each other since birth and are inseparable.

Exercising is a lot more bearable when you do it with a buddy.

A dog takes a horse for a jaunt around a corral. The racehorse and the pooch love to jog together.

Buddies complete ewe.

A lamb rides in a donkey's saddlebag in southeast Turkey.

A good buddy is always up for tagging along on an adventure.

An iguana and a manta ray near Cartagena, Colombia, make a surprisingly good pair. The manta ray gives the iguana rides from dock to dock, and the iguana reciprocates by giving his friend snacks.

Don't worry, your buddy's got your back.

Lion cubs and a dog became fast friends while living together at a vet's house outside Kiev, Ukraine.

Buddies like to horse around.

This macaw enjoys the view from the top of her buddy's head in Hamburg, Germany. She roams the countryside eating apples, playing with the family dog, and visiting the nearby horse barn where she helps groom the horses' manes and hitches rides.

Buddies of different feathers flock together.

Shelduck babies hitch a ride on Goosey, the Cape Barren goose, in the Wellington Zoo in New Zealand. Goosey wasn't able to have chicks of her own so zookeepers gave her some Shelduck eggs to raise and now she loves the ducklings like a mother.

A buddy would never claw you in the back.

A cat accompanies a miniature donkey as he grazes on a small farm. Even as a kitten she liked to sit on the donkey's back while he roamed the pasture.

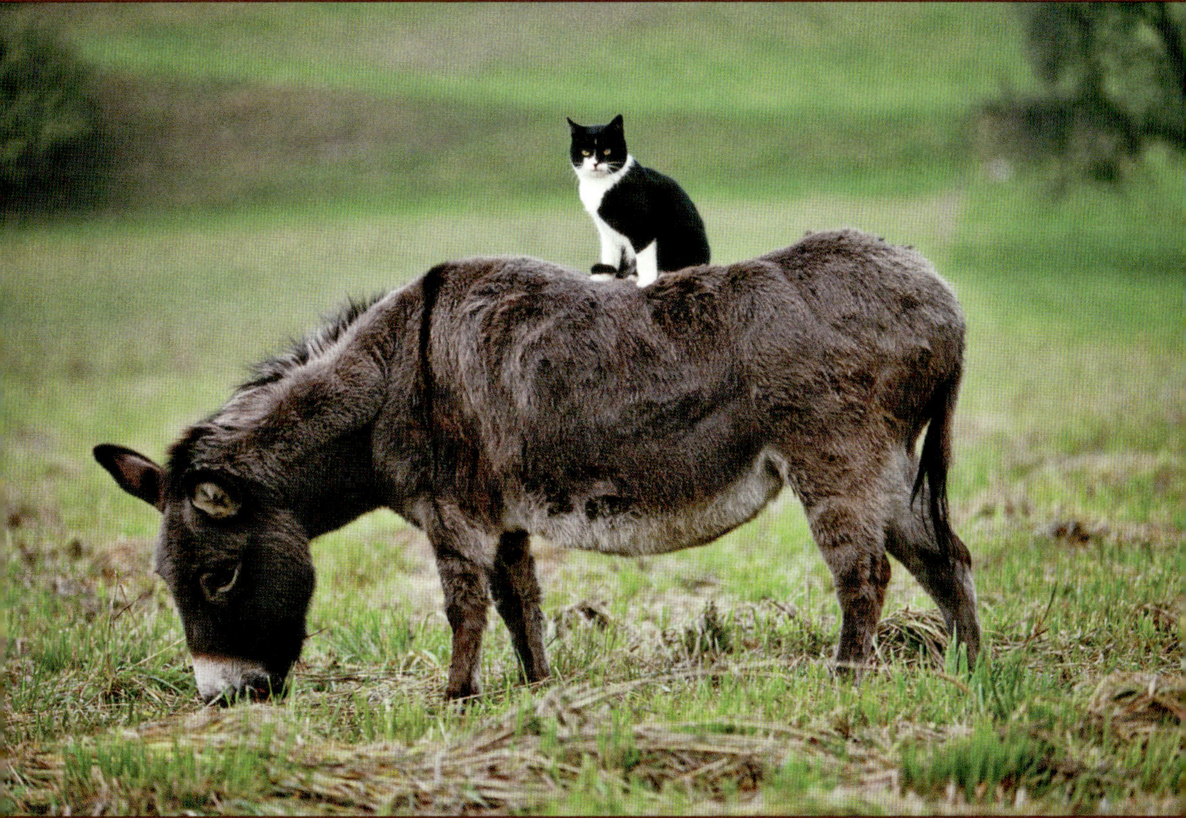

Buddies support you, even when your fashion choices are questionable.

Keow Wan the parrot hitches a ride on canine pal Yim's head in Thailand. The friends' owners fashioned Yim's special hat so Keow Wan could ride in style and Yim could transport him in comfort.

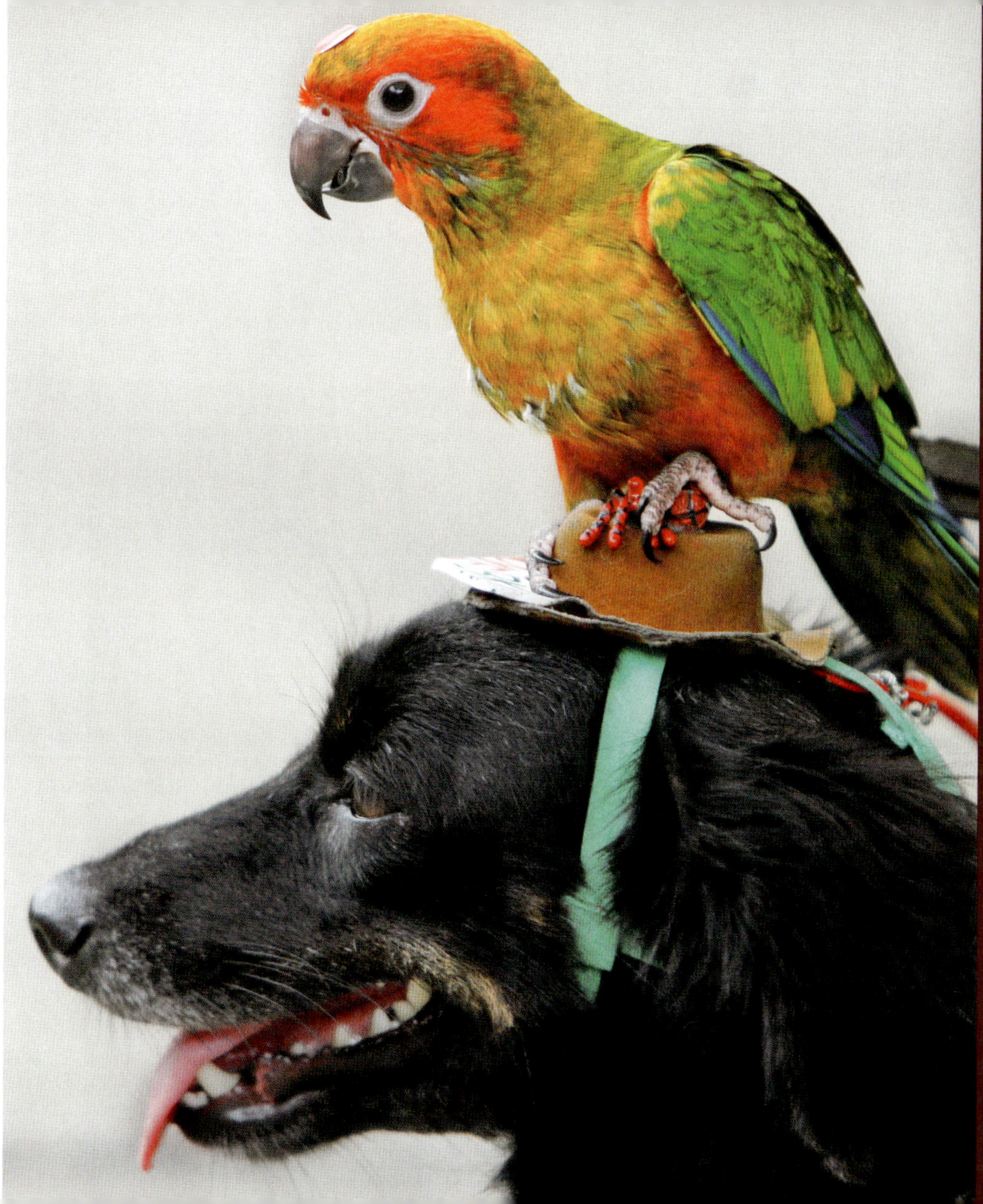

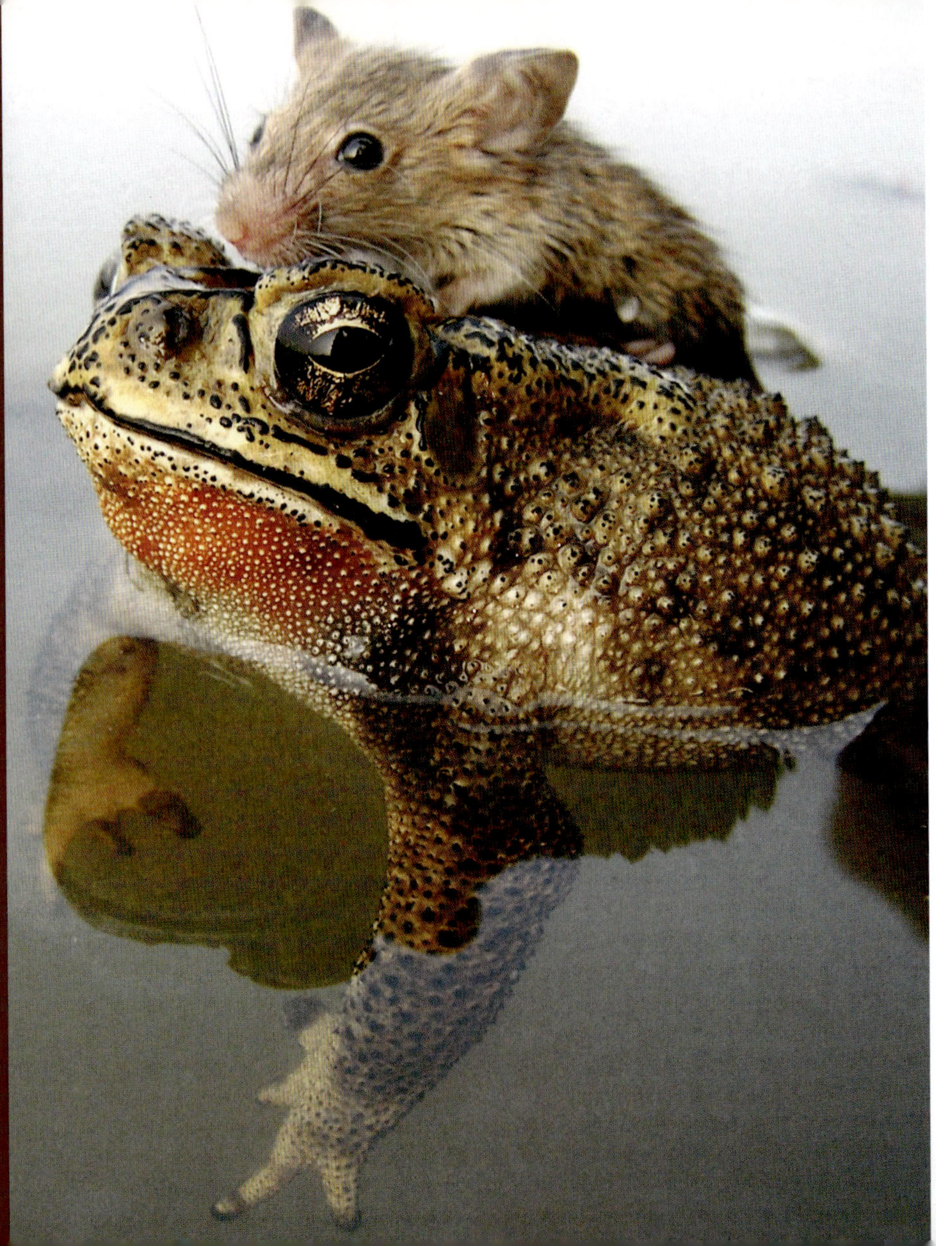

A buddy will help you when you feel like you're drowning.

A courageous frog swam a mouse to safety through floodwaters in the northern Indian city of Lucknow.

A buddy lets you know when you don't look so hot.

A monkey dressed in traditional clothing grooms a parrot at a wild-animal park in southern China. The characters on the monkey's cap mean "Buddha," and since this pair has been together they have been at peace with the world.

37

Buddies don't eat you, even when they totally could.

A donkey, who was intended to be a meal for a wolf, now shares an enclosure with his sharp-toothed friend in Albania.

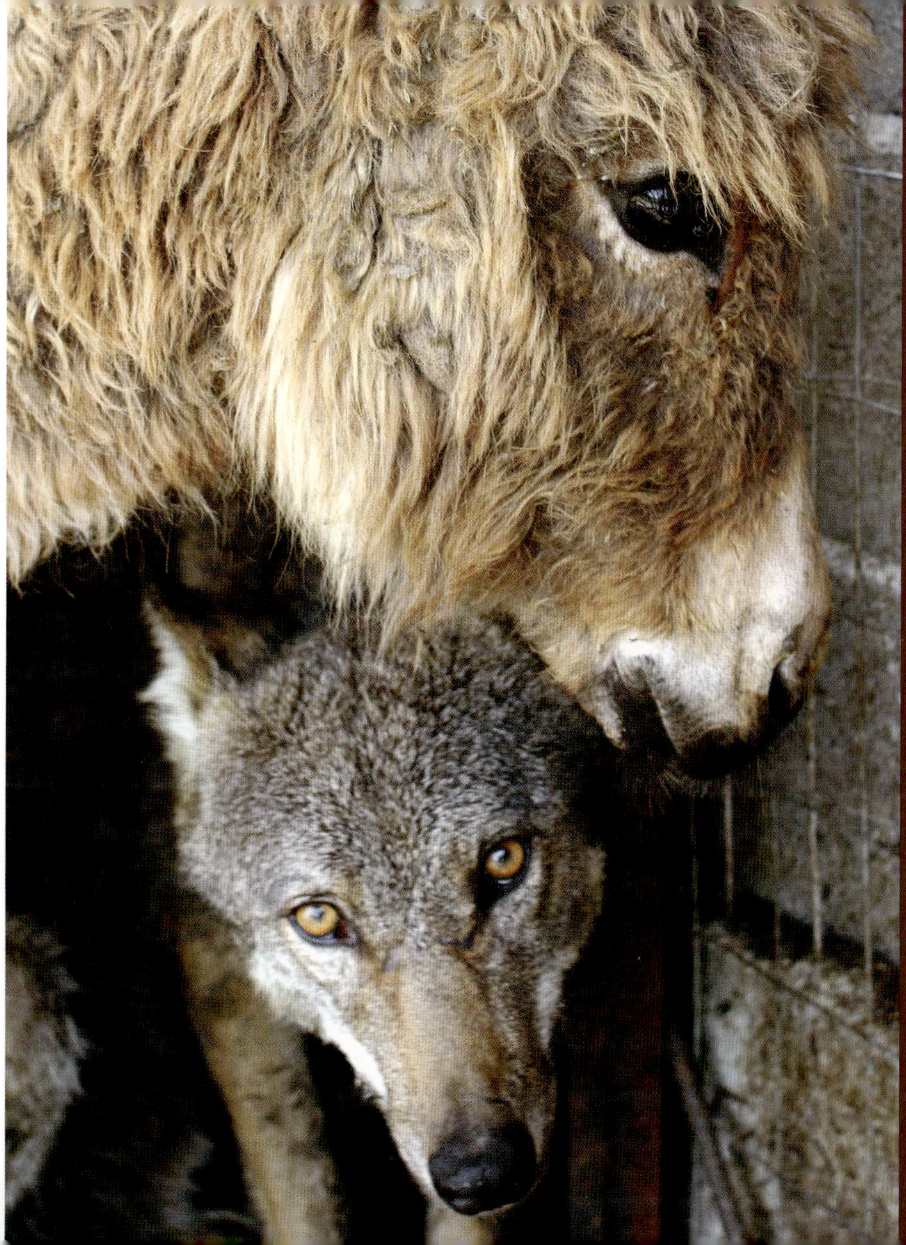

Being buddies can simply be a matter of sharing the same tastes.

Clover the rhino and Bok-Bok the goat, both orphans living on the Rhino & Lion Nature Reserve near Johannesburg, South Africa, bond over a shared love of horse pellets. Mmmmm.

41

42

Buddies know when you need a fuzzy nuzzle.

Ikura, a pug, enjoys a little love from Gari, a minipig, in Tokyo, Japan. Ikura and Gari have been best buds since Gari became part of the family.

We all need some*buddy* to lean on.

BoonLua, a long-tailed macaque, rests his head on Toby the rabbit in his enclosure near Bangkok, Thailand. BoonLua lost his legs and one arm during a dog attack and managed to drag himself to a temple, where he was treated. Toby doesn't mind being a headrest when BoonLua needs to take a load off.

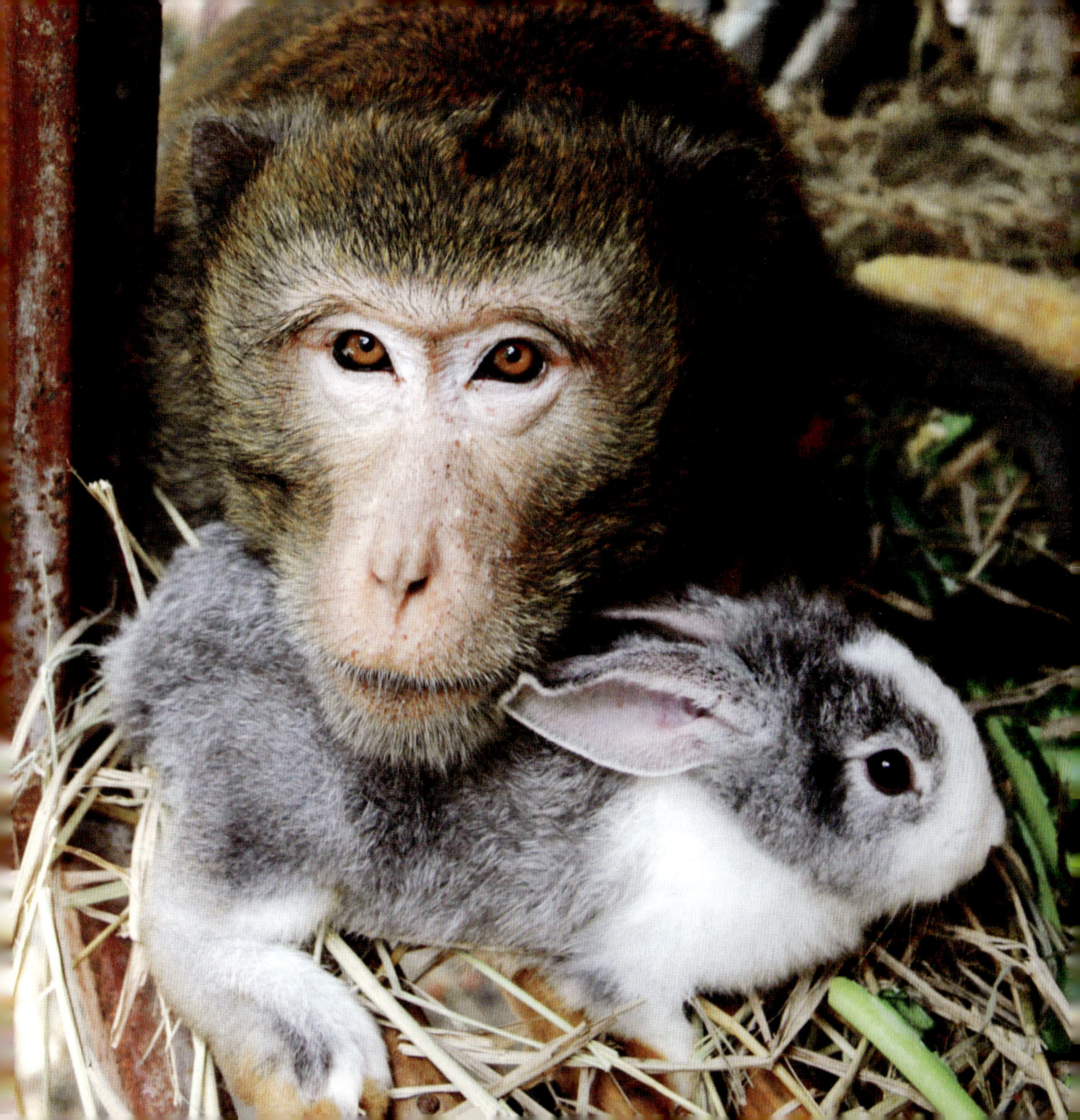

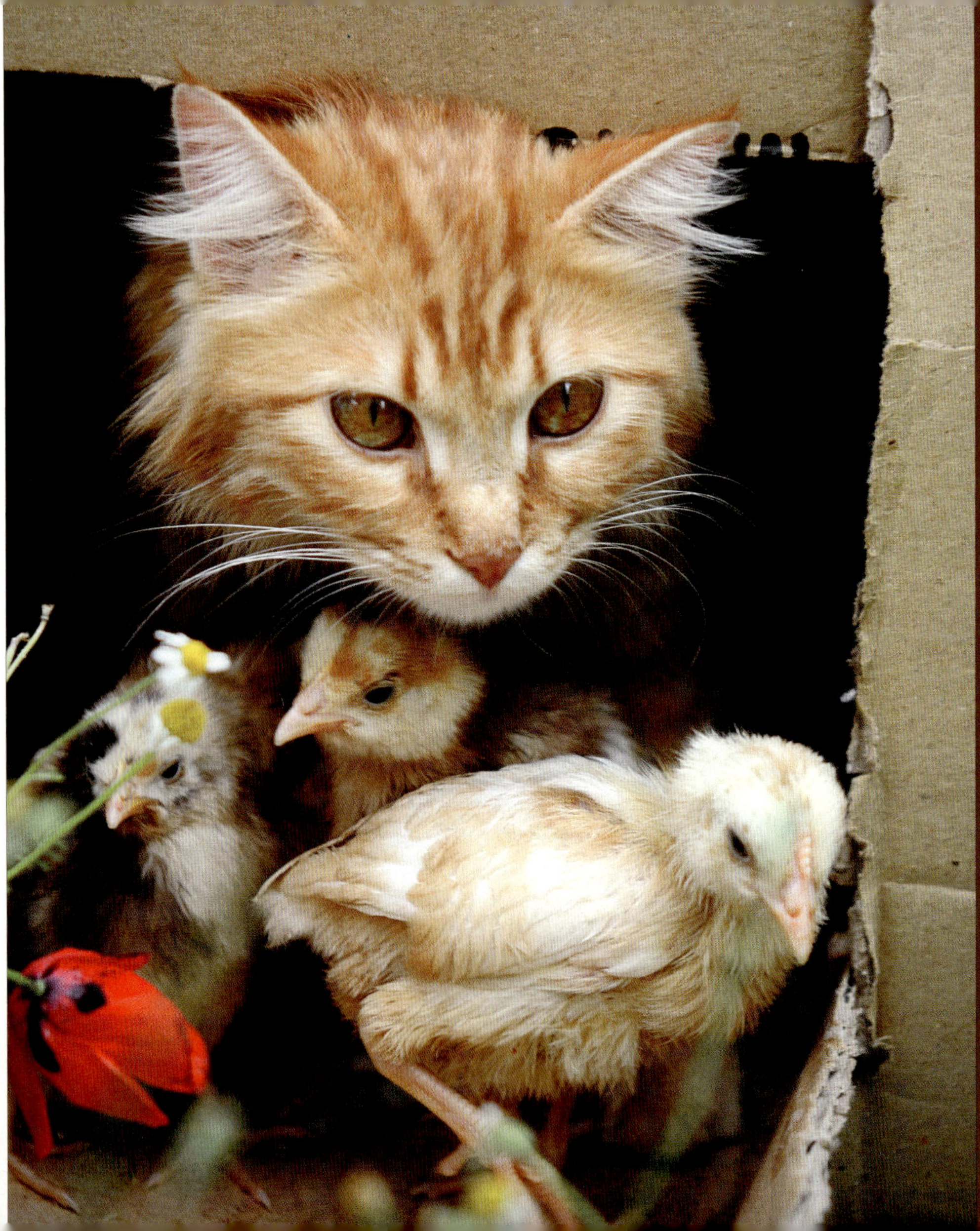

Buddies enjoy playing chicken.

Nimra the cat became a surrogate mother for seven chicks in Amman, Jordan, after their mother passed away. She rarely thinks they look delicious.

Buddies high-five!

Tangchil the dog plays with longtime roommate Soonee the lioness at a zoo near Seoul, South Korea.

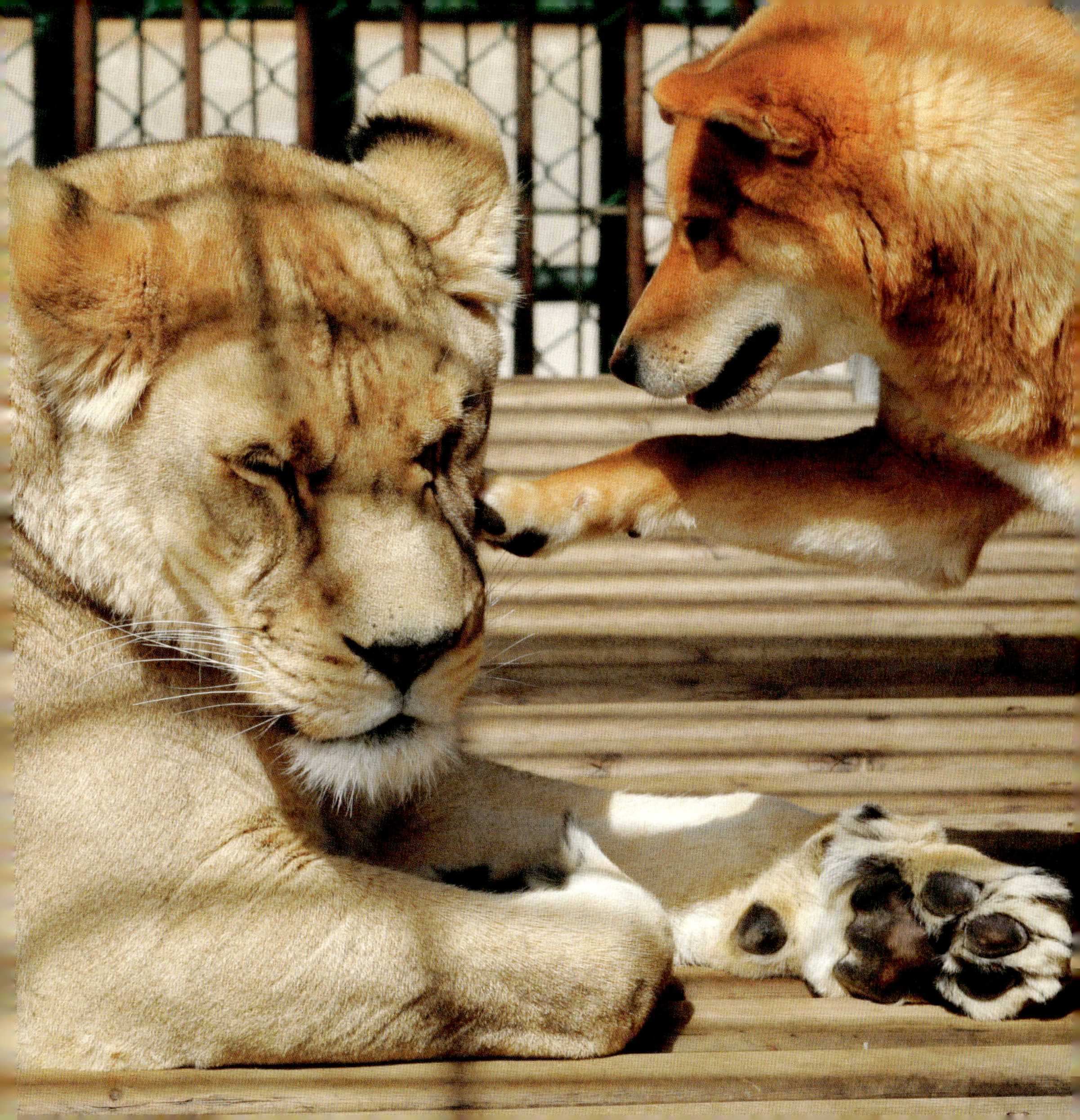

Buddies are impressed if you can touch your nose with your tongue.

A French bulldog gives a tiger cub an affectionate lick at a zoo in southern Japan. The Bengal tiger was abandoned by its mother and now the bulldog is raising the cub as if it were her own.

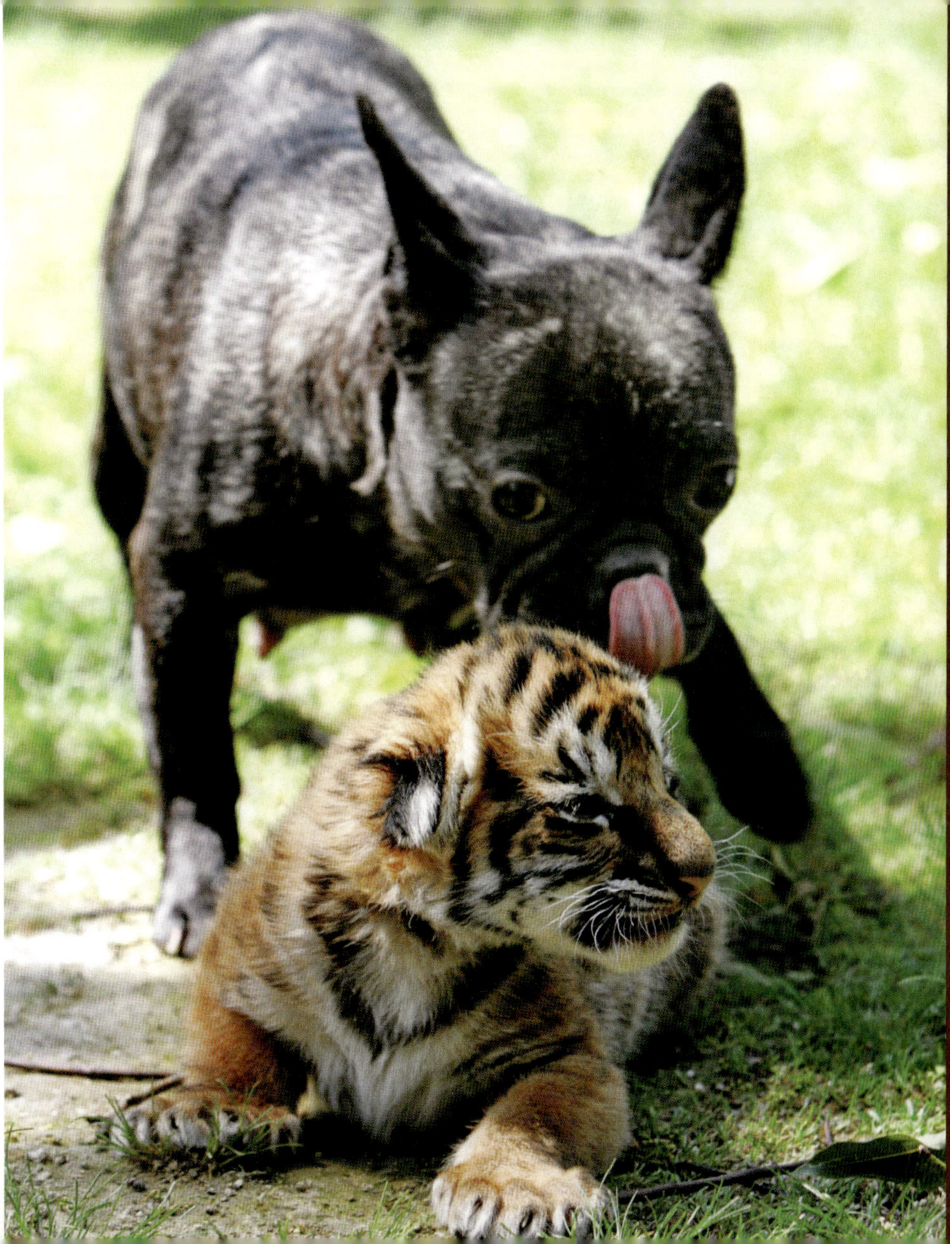

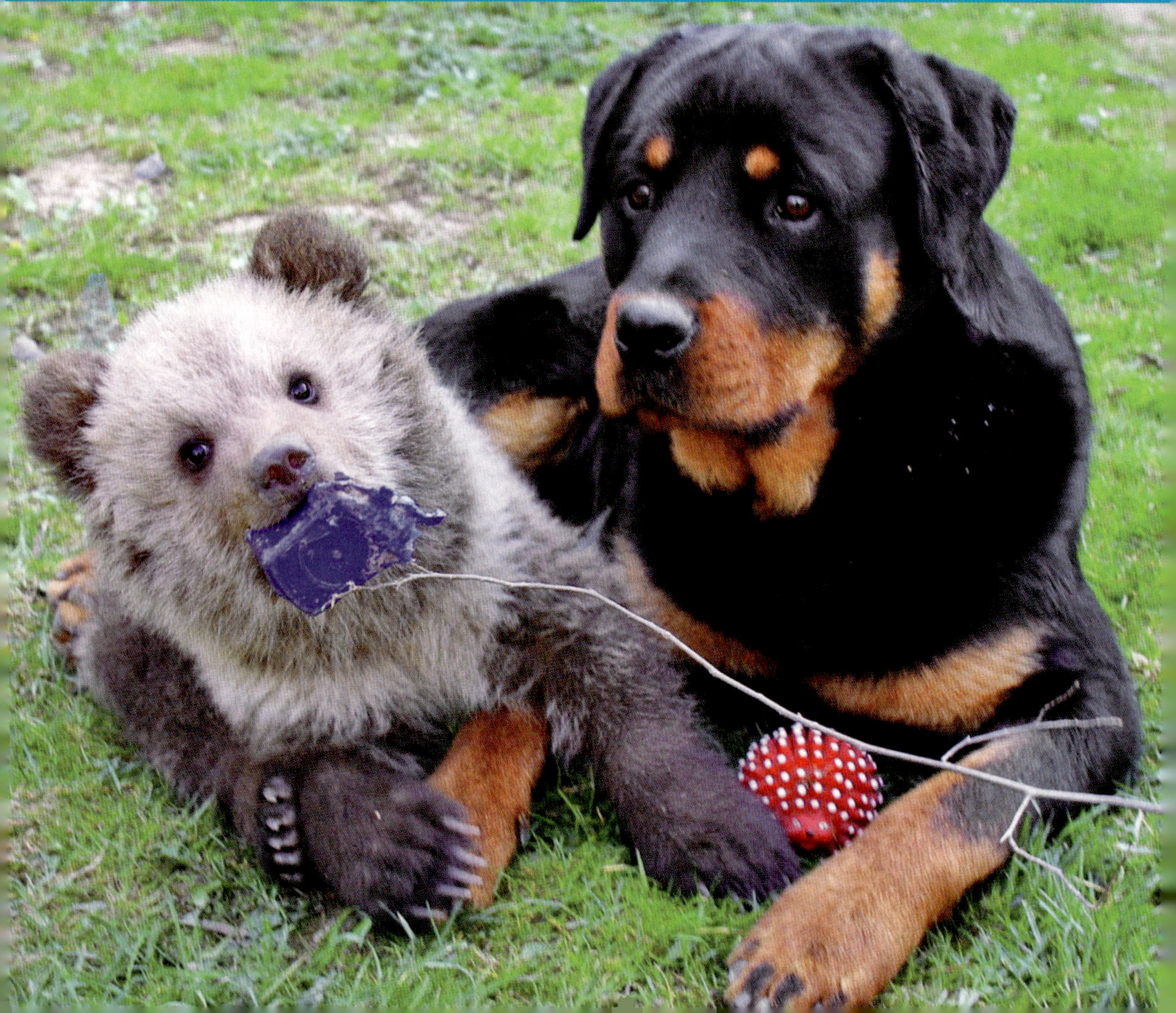

Sometimes buddies start to look like one another.

A young Rottweiler buddies up to his brown bear cub pal in Košice, Slovakia. Along with its four siblings, the cub was separated from its mother after six weeks and relies on the Rottweiler for protection and companionship.

Buddies can have a nose for certain things.

Charles the giant rabbit snogs his best friend William the miniature pig at Pennywell Farm in Devon, England. When William was ten weeks old he was introduced to Charles, and now wherever Charles goes William follows.

55

56

When looking for a new buddy, remember that polar opposites can attract.

A sled dog and a polar bear share a quiet moment in the frozen tundra of Canada. The polar bear approached the huskies and instead of attacking, the animals began to play with each other. For the next week the polar bear would come at dusk and visit his new friends.

Buddies don't carp at you.

A black swan delivers food to some carp at a wildlife park in Guangdong, China, on a regular basis. Like a mama bird feeding her young, she stores food pellets and places them in the mouths of the fish.

59

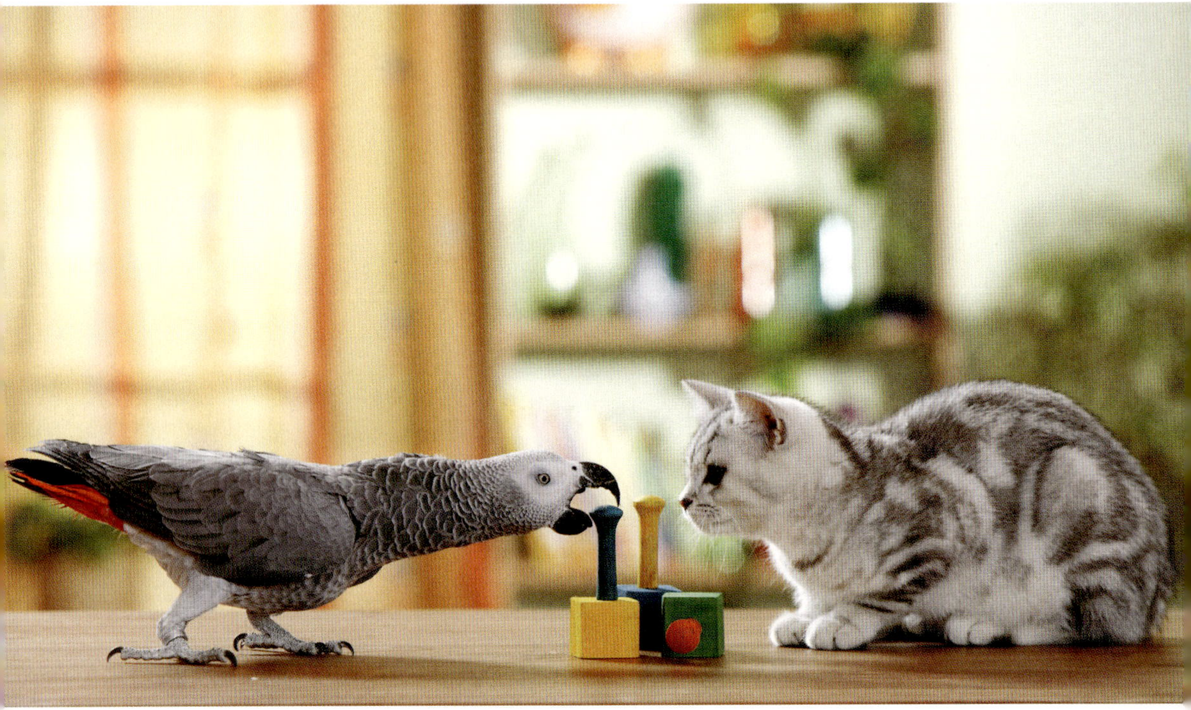

Buddies will let you win one every once in a while.

An African gray parrot plays a move against a British shorthair cat in their home in northern England. The two pets, though natural enemies, get along splendidly.

Real buddies turn the other cheek.

This capybara demurely ignores the fact that his squirrel monkey friend is sticking his tongue out at him, at a zoo near Tokyo, Japan.

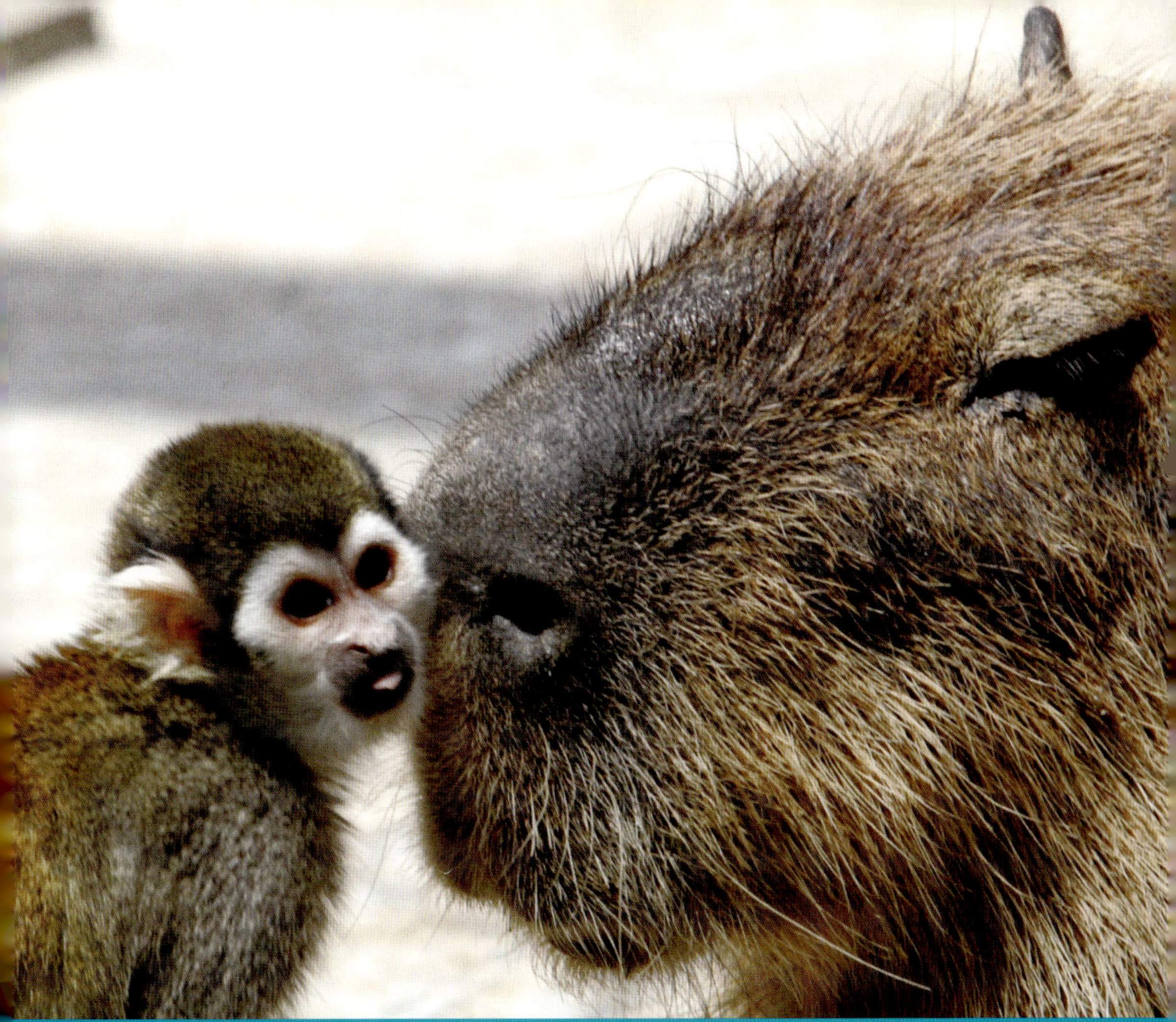

It's okay to size up a new buddy—just try to be subtle about it.

A Norfolk terrier and a donkey size one another up while out on the farm. The small dog has befriended many of the farm's animals, following them as they look for food.

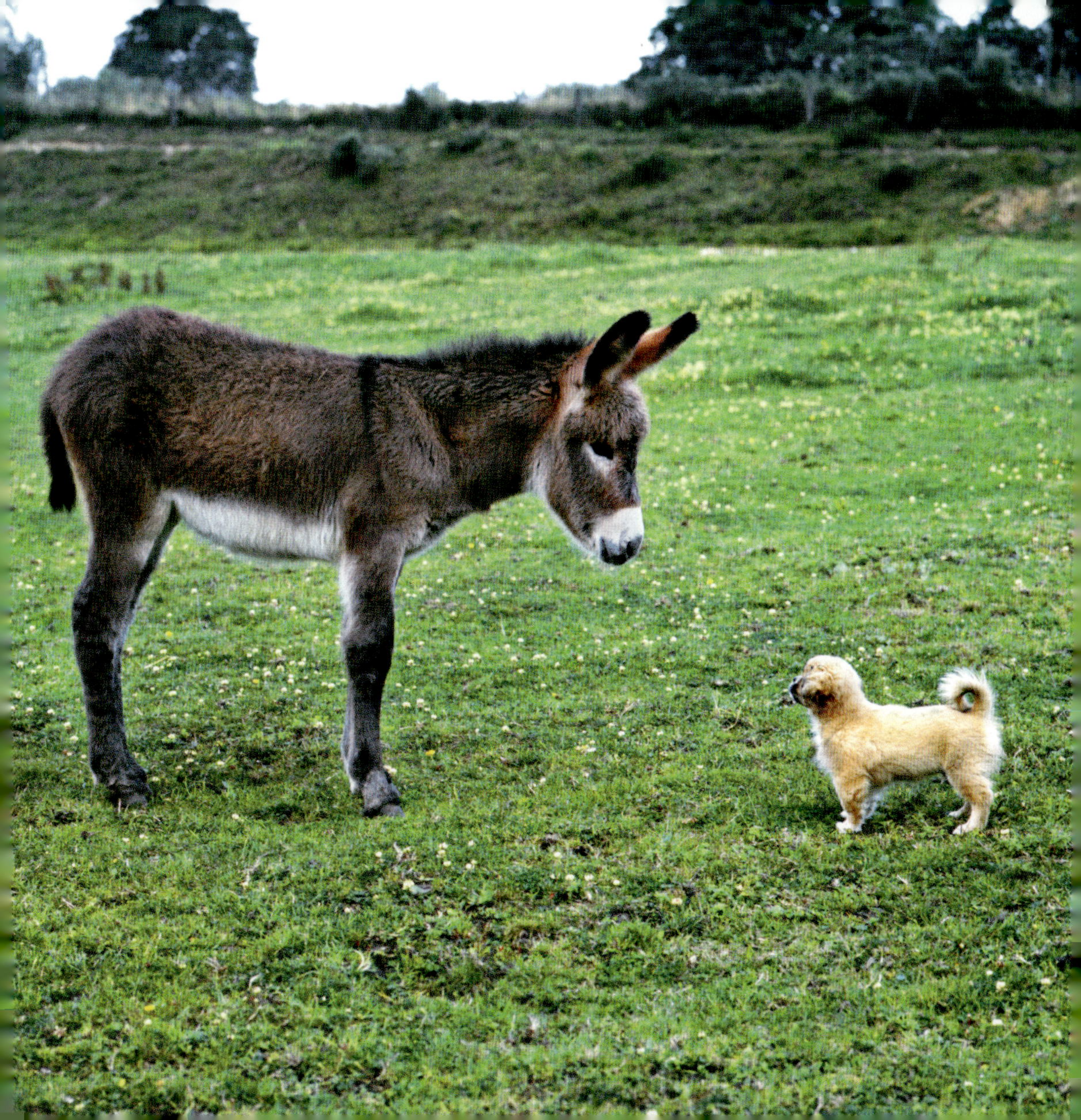

Buddies don't care if you're fat or thin, fast or slow.

Mzee, a giant male Aldabran tortoise, took baby hippo Owen under his wing after Owen was rescued by game wardens and settled at Kenya's Haller Park animal sanctuary. They are an inseparable twosome.

67

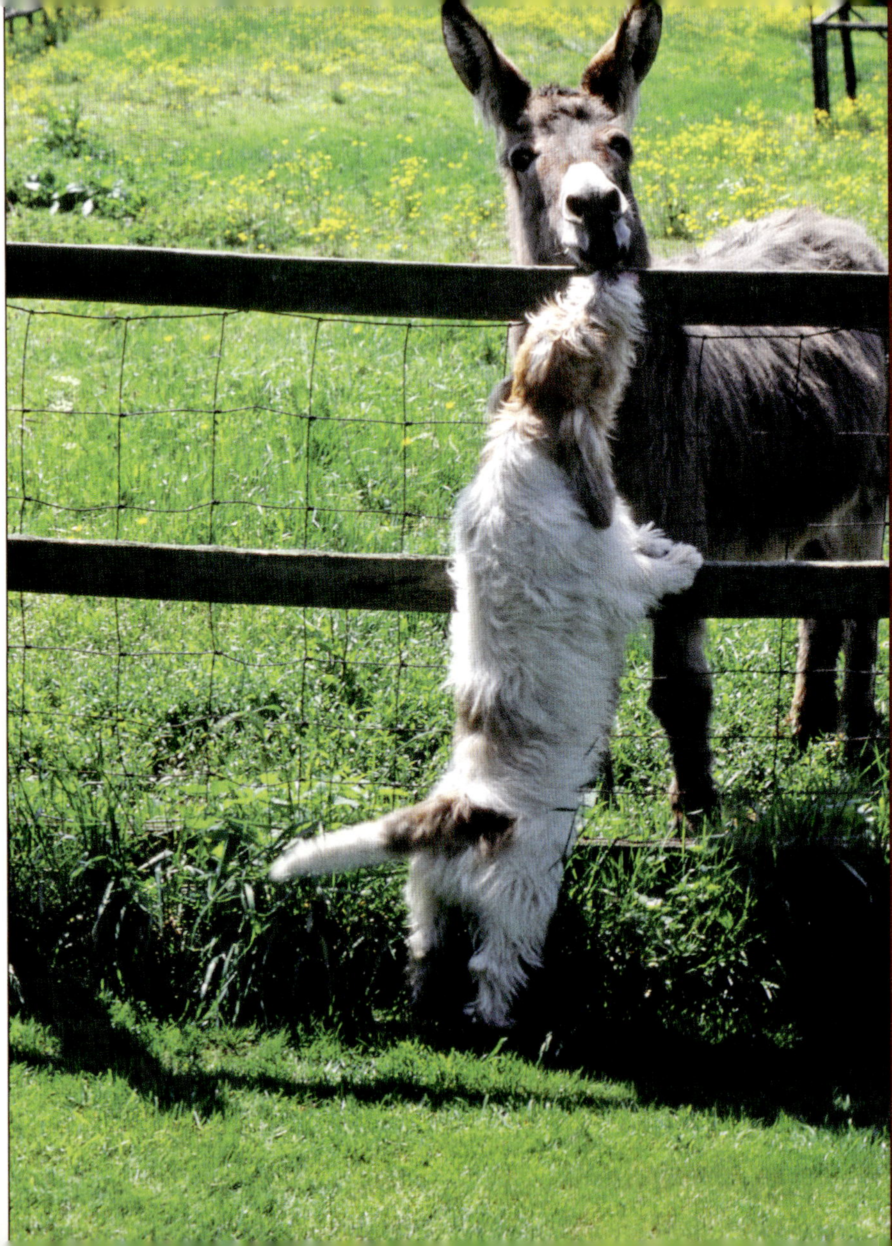

Buddies meet you halfway.

A sheepdog reaches for a kiss from his donkey buddy at a farm.

It's okay if the cat's got your tongue when you're with a buddy.

Auan the cat has looked after Jeena the mouse ever since Auan discovered Jeena in his farmhouse near Bangkok, Thailand.

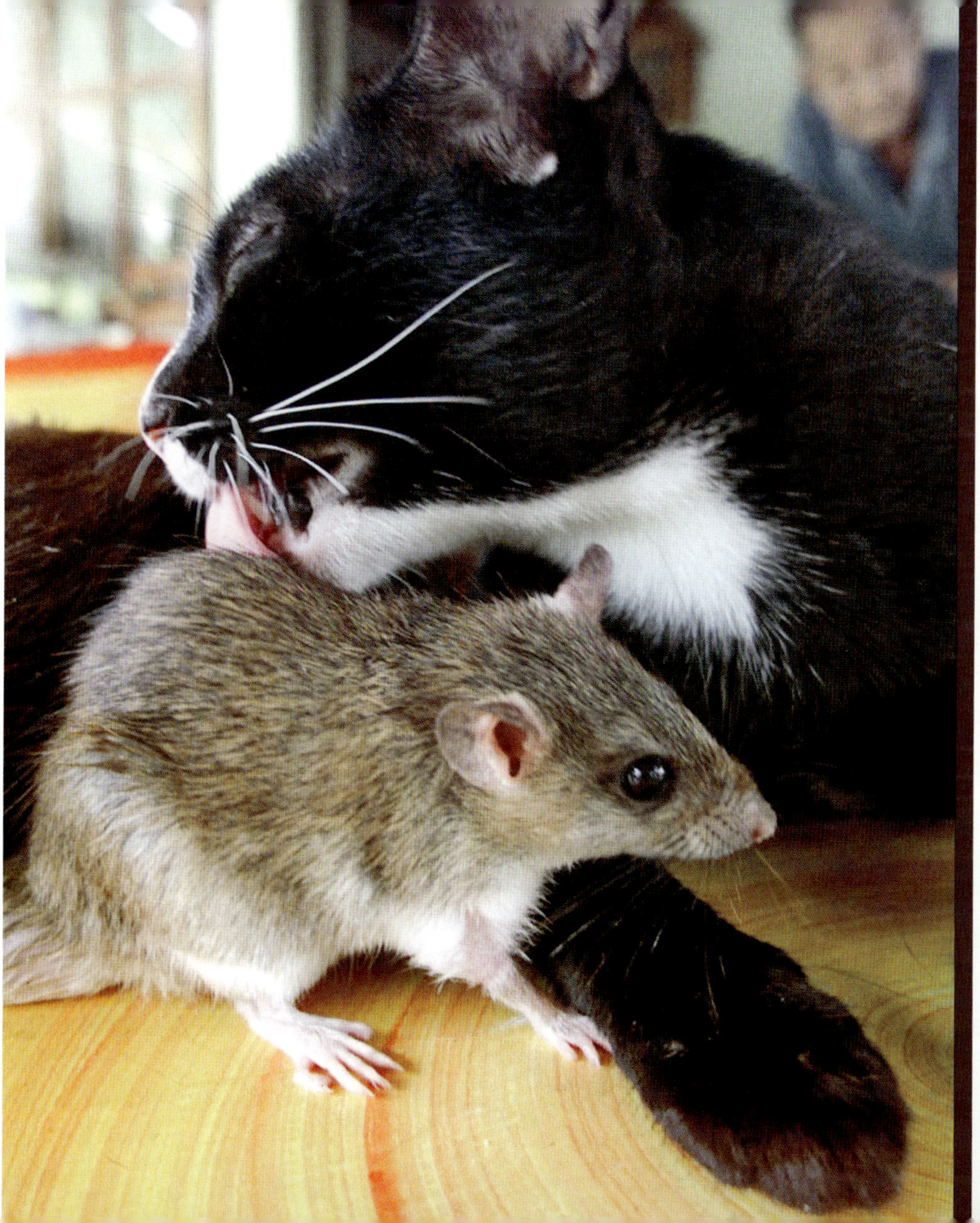

Buddies make prime*mates.*

Best buds Suryia the orangutan and Roscoe the bluetick coonhound go on walks, eat, and swim together at the T.I.G.E.R.S. sanctuary in Myrtle Beach, South Carolina.

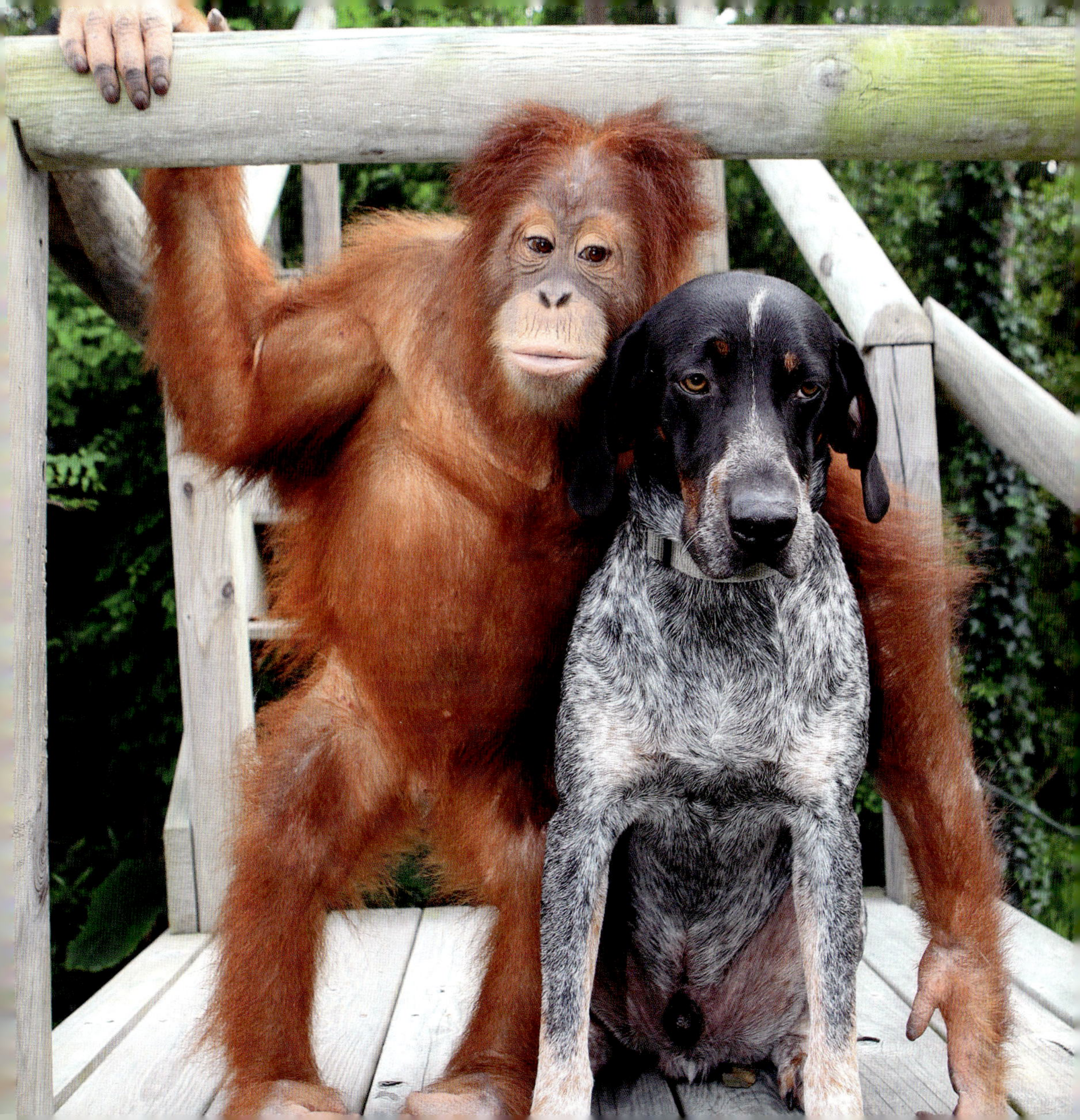

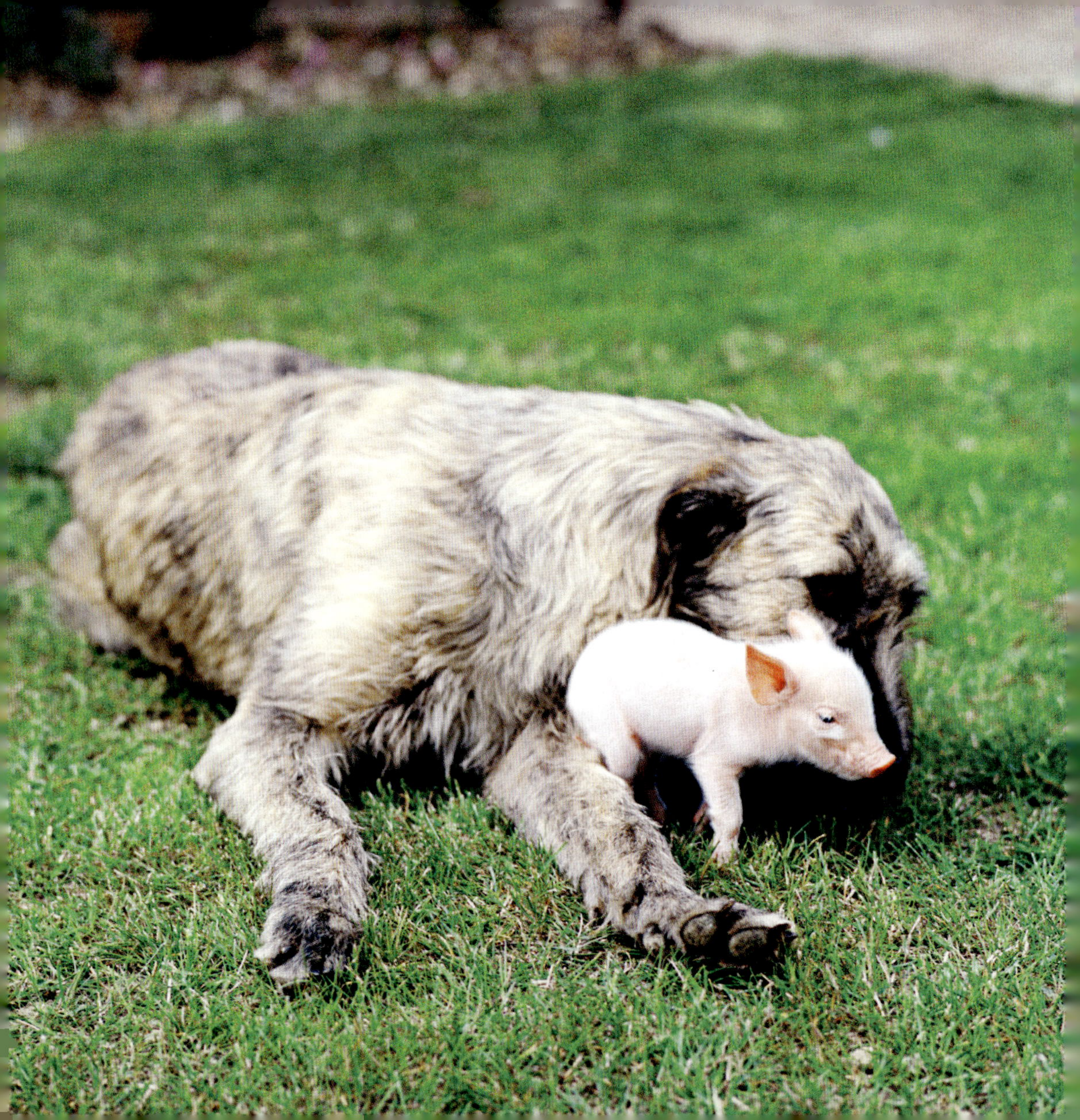

Buddies pig out together.

A piglet snuggles with its shaggy canine pal in the grass.

Never cheetah buddy.

Lisha, a Labrador, raises Josh and Jordan, two cheetah cubs. Lisha, who has never had puppies of her own, has raised more than thirty animal orphans, ranging from anteaters to zebras, at the Cango Wildlife Ranch in South Africa.

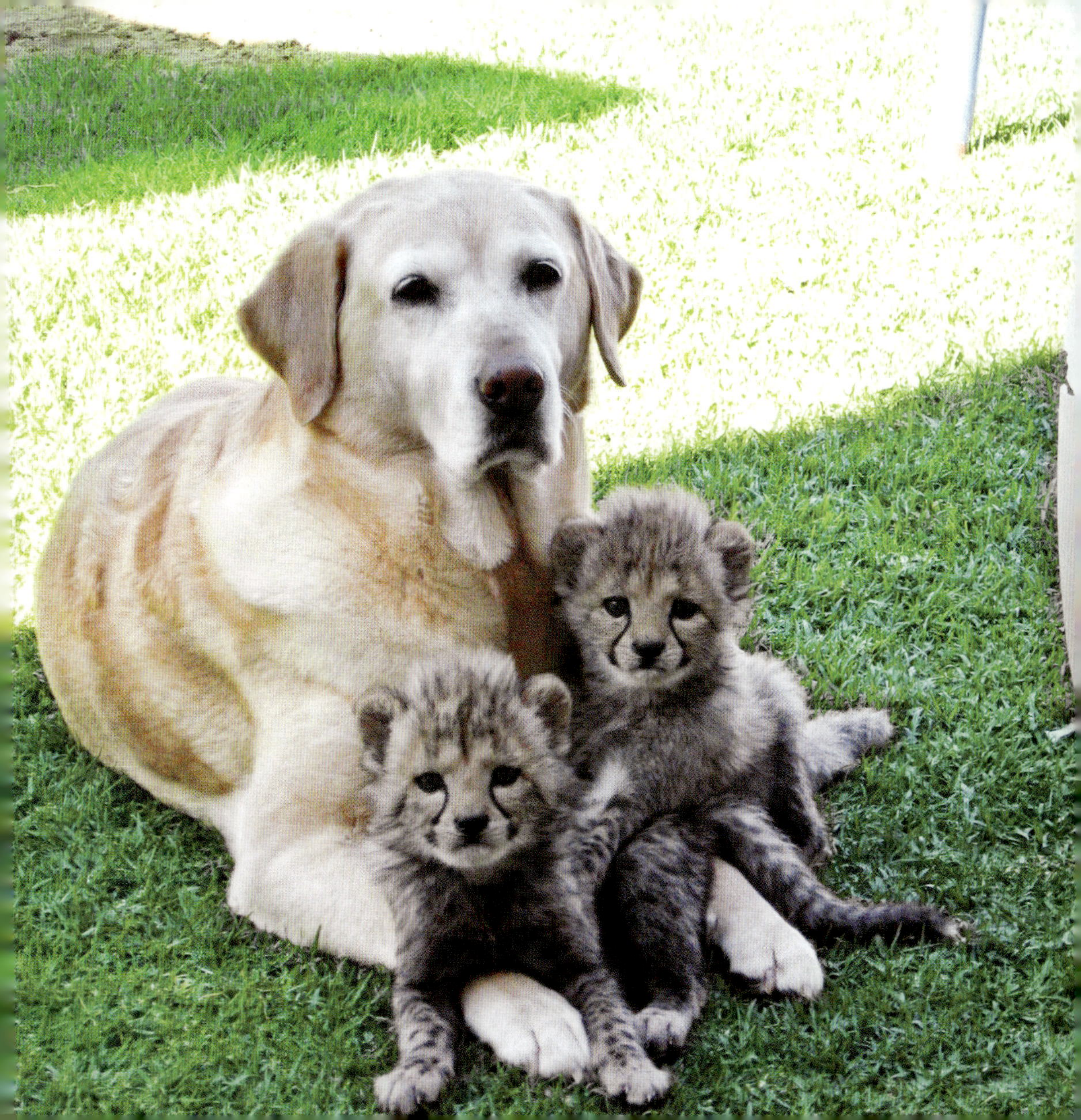

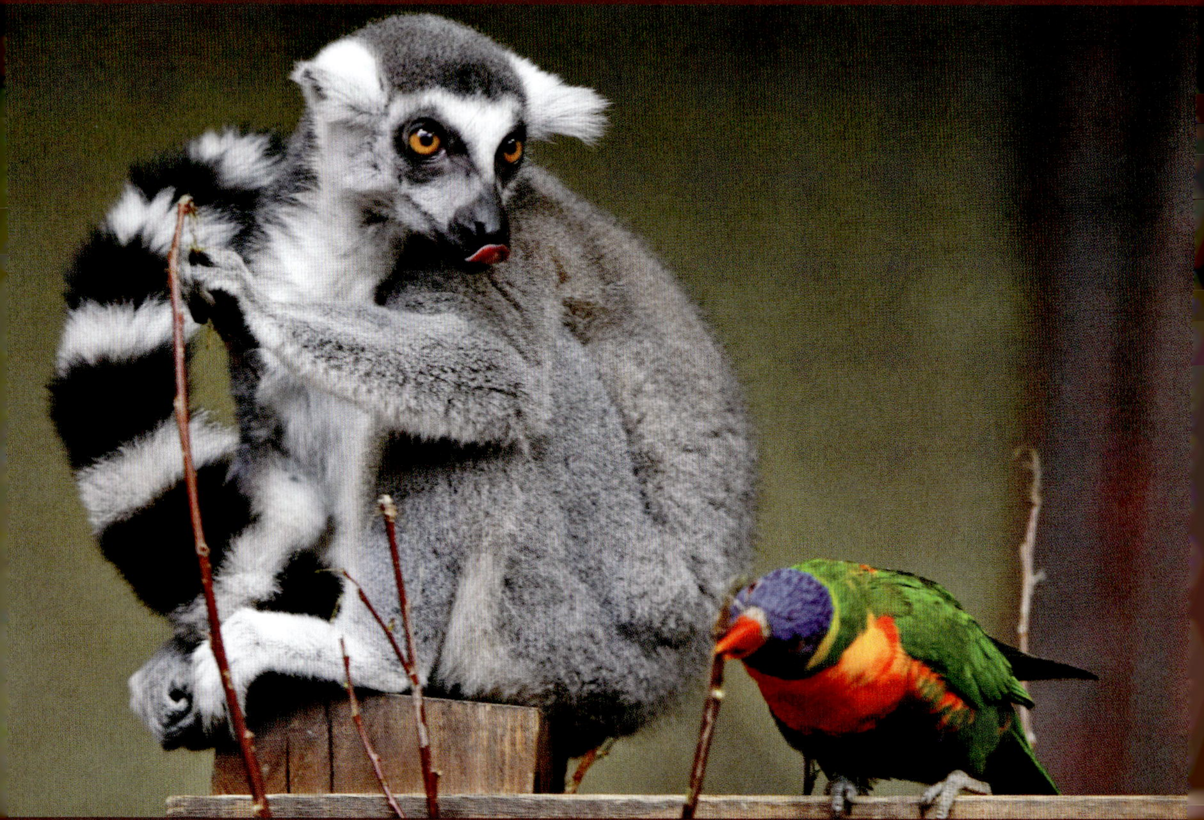

Some buddies see the world in black and white, others see it in color.

A ring-tailed lemur and a colorful parrot enjoy each other's company. The two live in the same enclosure in a zoo in Hamburg, Germany.

A buddy will needle you when necessary.

A baby raccoon plays with a porcupine in a field. Even though they're having fun, the raccoon knows not to let his bud get too close!

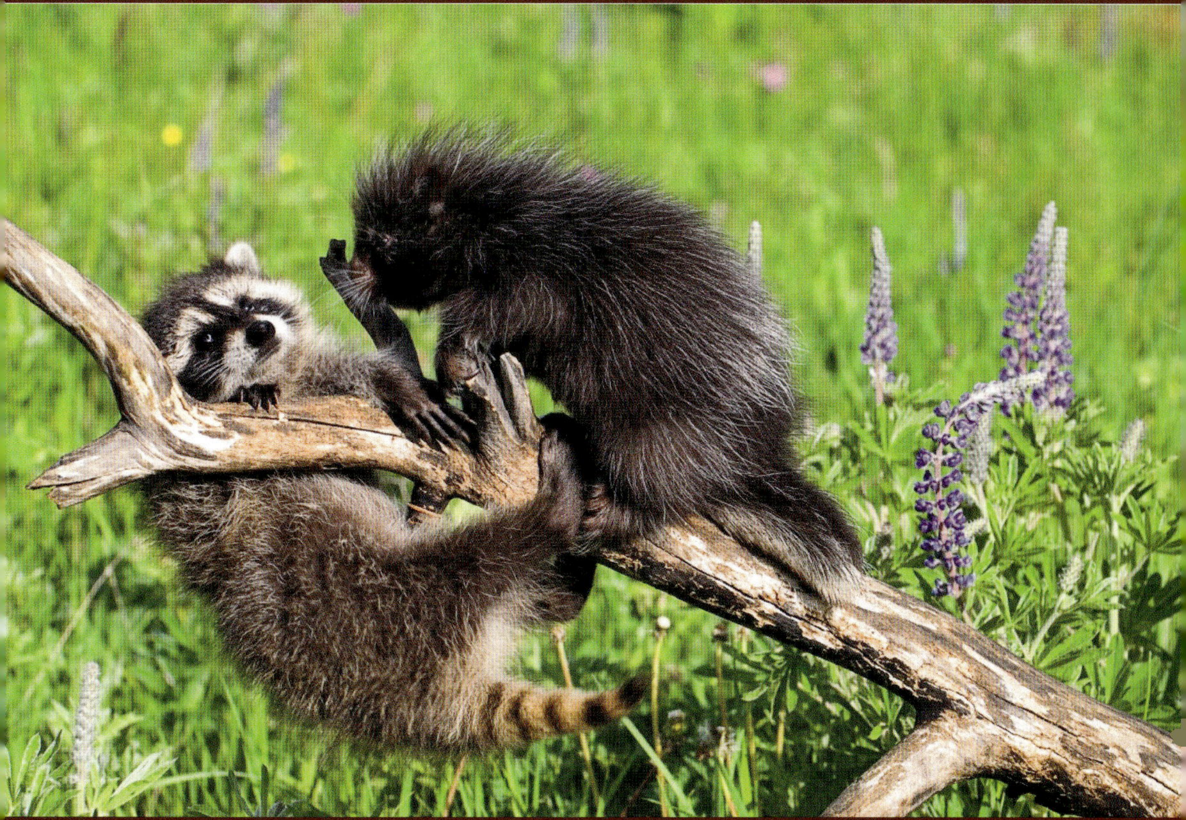

Buddies stick by you even when you're a basket case.

After being found and nursed to health by a hunter, this abandoned wild boar piglet befriended the man's hunting dogs and plays with them in his garden in Germany.

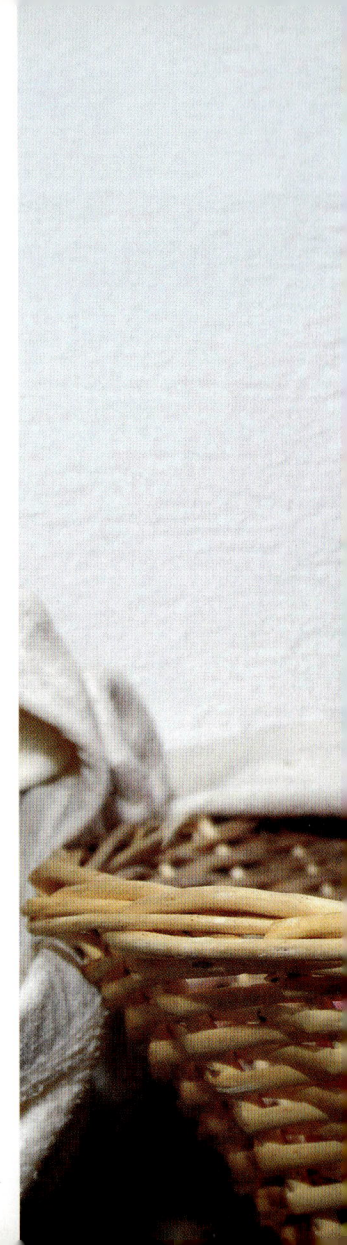

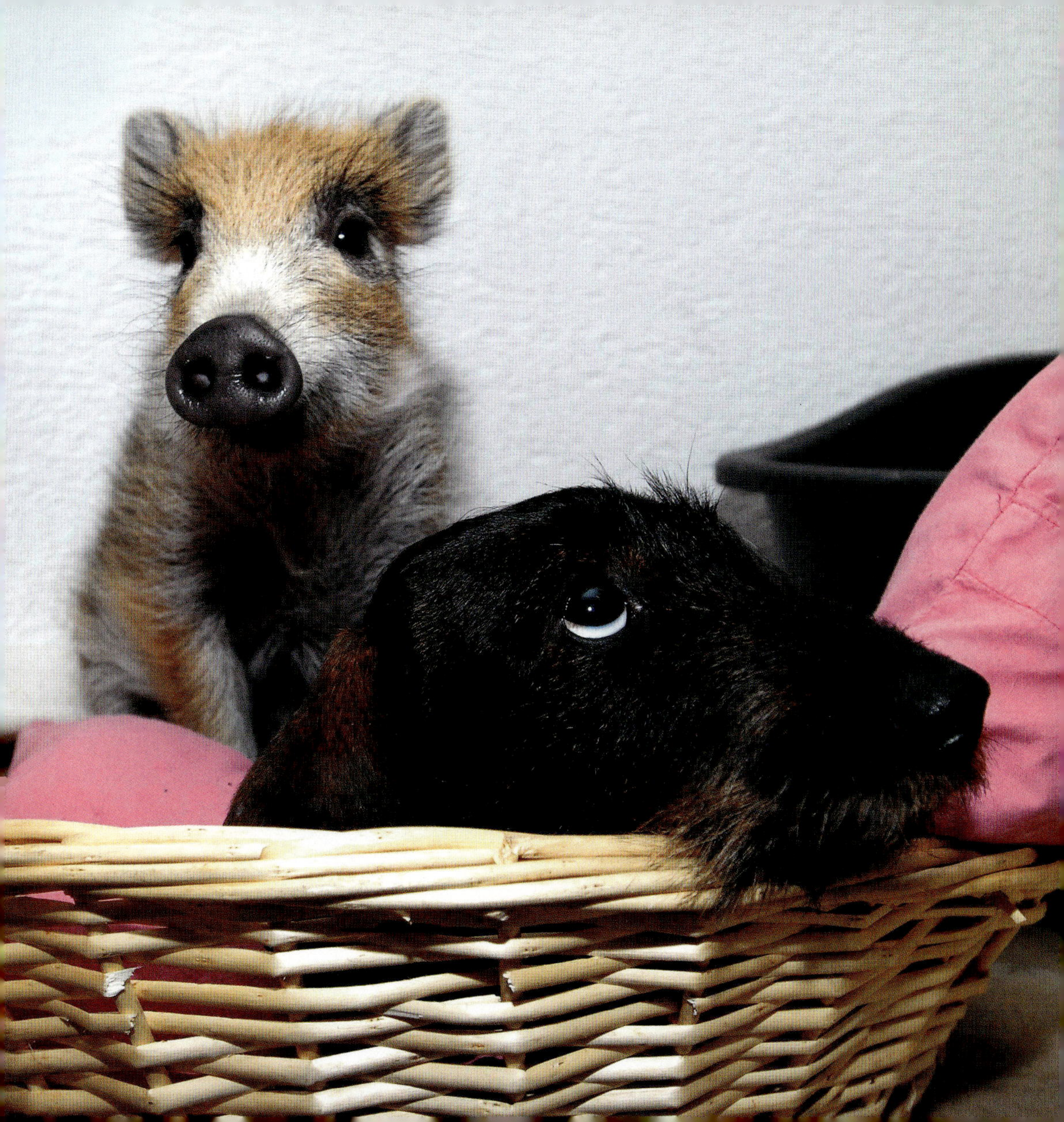

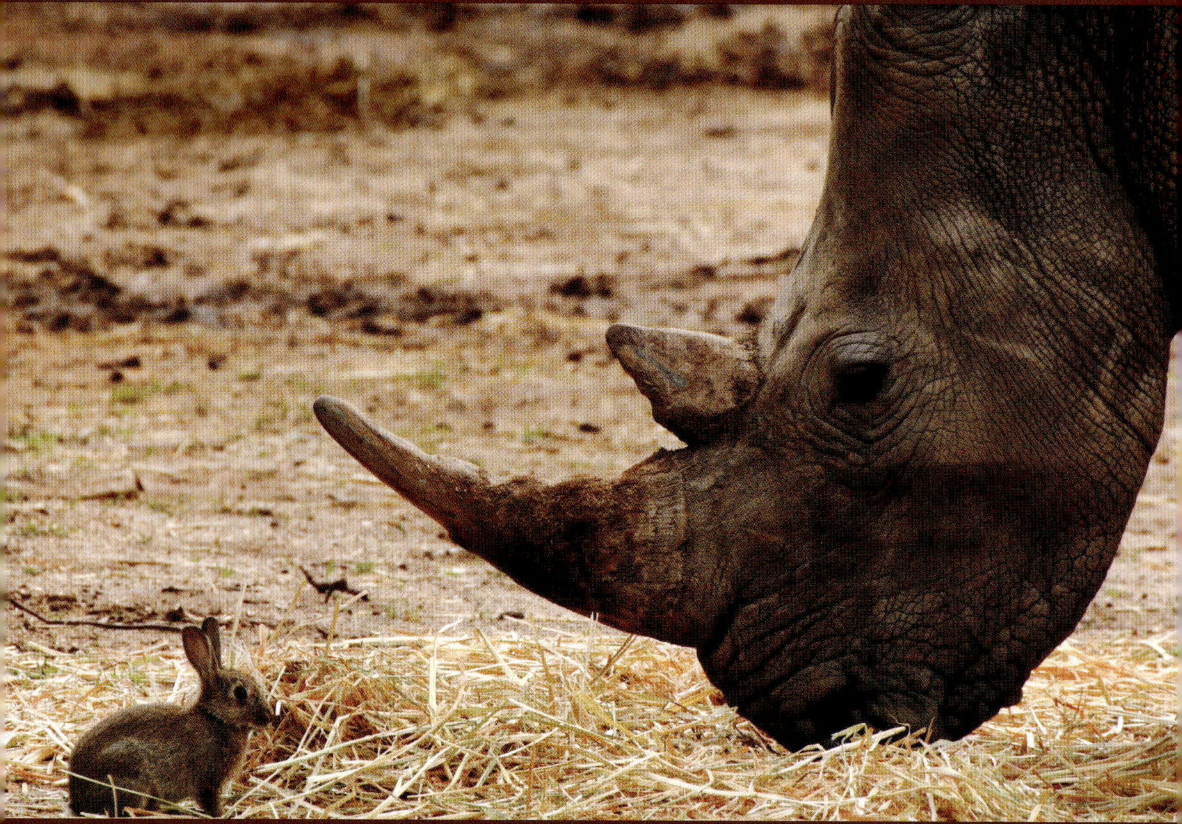

When it comes to buddies, size doesn't matter.

This tiny rabbit isn't intimidated by Umqali, the large white rhino at the Taronga Western Plains Zoo in Sydney, Australia. The little guy, who isn't even part of the zoo, hopped into the rhino's enclosure one day and now visits regularly, sometimes sleeping next to his best friend.

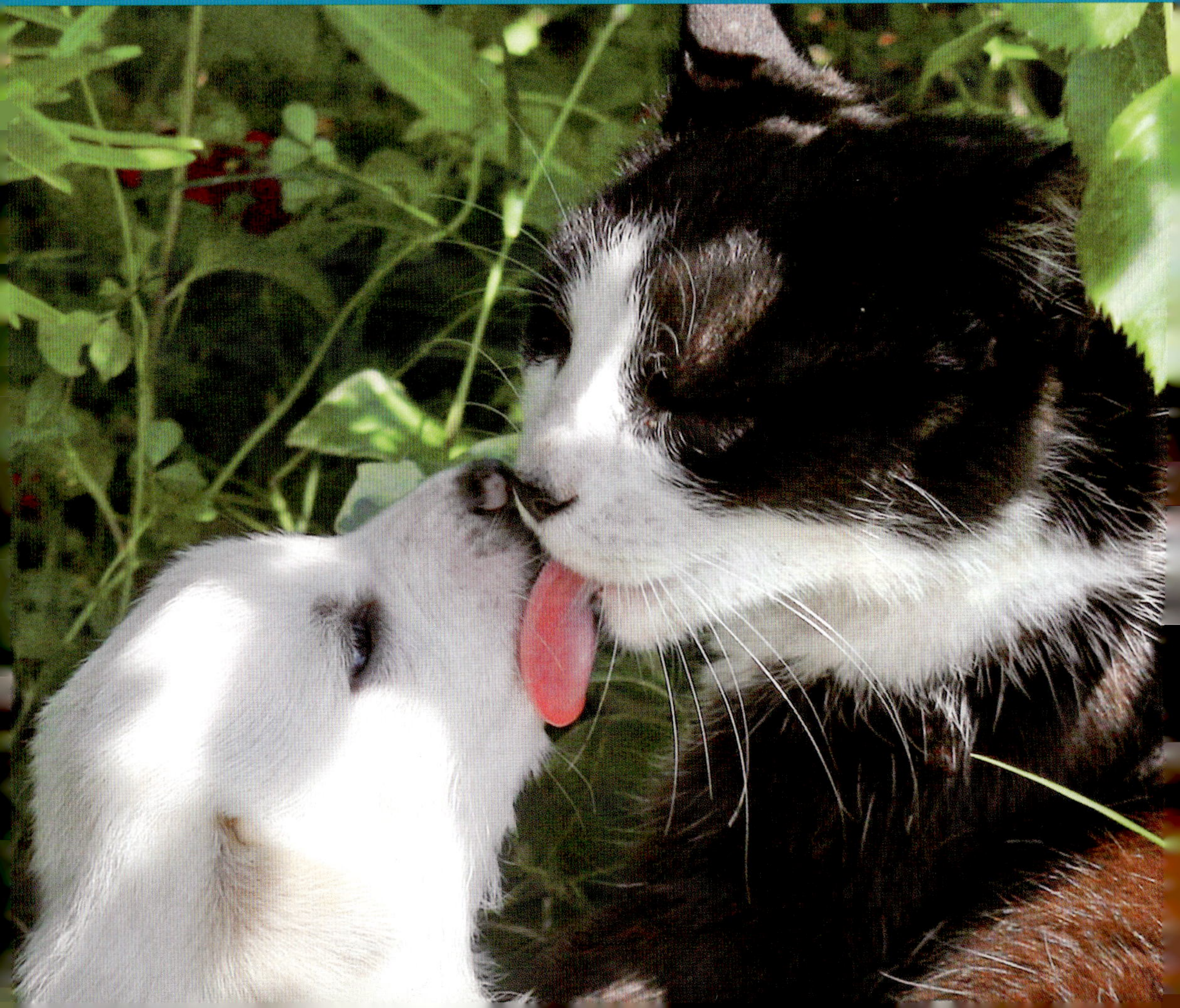

Buddies let you know if you have something on your face. *Good* buddies remove it!

A cat who lost her kitten in an accident grooms a puppy who was orphaned after his mother was hit by a car near the city of Tirana, Albania.

Sometimes you and your buddy just have to hug it out.

A macaque hugs his best bud, a white pigeon, on Neilingding Island and Futian Nature Reserve, off the coast of southern China. The tiny monkey wandered away from his mother but was luckily found by an animal protection group and given a new home, where a pigeon lived nearby. The two became instant friends.

89

Photo Credits:

1. Fotosearch
2. BARCROFT MEDIA/Fame Pictures
3. BARCROFT MEDIA/Fame Pictures
4. BARCROFT MEDIA/ Fame Pictures
5. Animal Photography/Sally Anne Thompson
6. REUTERS/China Daily
7. Koichi Kamoshida/Getty Images
8. Melanie Stetson Freeman/The Christian Science Monitor/Getty Images
9. BARCROFT MEDIA/Fame Pictures
10. Fotosearch/Juniors Bildarchive
11. REUTERS/Fatih Saribas
12. REUTERS/Fredy Builes
13. REUTERS/Gleb Garanich
14. BARCROFT MEDIA/Fame Pictures
15. BARCROFT MEDIA/Fame Pictures
16. NHPA Photoshot/ Manfred Danegger
17. REUTERS/Chaiwat Subprasom
18. REUTERS/Pawan Kumar
19. REUTERS/China Daily
20. REUTERS/Arben Celi
21. REUTERS/Ed Stoddard
22. REUTERS/Eriko Sugita
23. REUTERS/Sukree Sukplang
24. REUTERS/Ali Jarekji
25. REUTERS/You Sung-Ho
26. REUTERS/Yuriko Nakao
27. REUTERS/STR New
28. BARCROFT MEDIA/Fame Pictures
29. World Pictures/Photoshot
30. REUTERS/China Daily
31. Fotosearch/Juniors Bildarchive
32. REUTERS/Kim Kyung-Hoon
33. Animal Photography/Sally Anne Thompson
34. REUTERS/Peter Greste
35. Animal Photography/Sally Anne Thompson
36. REUTERS/Sukree Sukplang
37. BARCROFT MEDIA/Fame Pictures
38. Animal Photography/Sally Anne Thompson
39. BARCROFT MEDIA/Fame Pictures
40. REUTERS/Christian Charisius
41. Fotosearch
42. BARCROFT Media/Fame Pictures
43. ICONX/Fame Pictures
44. REUTERS/Arben Celi
45. CNImaging/Photoshot/Huojb